THE OFFICIAL DUFFER'S RULES OF GOLF

BY JOHN NOBLE

CONTEMPORARY
BOOKS, INC.
CHICAGO

Published by Contemporary Books, Inc.
180 North Michigan Avenue, Chicago, Illinois 60601
Manufactured in the United States of America
International Standard Book Number: 0-8092-5144-2

Published simultaneously in Canada by Beaverbooks, Ltd.
195 Allstate Parkway, Valleywood Business Park
Markham, Ontario L3R 4T8 Canada

THE OFFICIAL DUFFER'S RULES OF GOLF

CONTENTS

PART ONE
ETIQUETTE

PART TWO
DEFINITIONS

PART THREE
THE RULES

PART FOUR
APPENDICES

ETIQUETTE

Preparing for the battle of the links

The Royal & Ancient Game of Golf is one helluva hard game. The dedicated and diligent duffer must not only deal with the demanding elements of the game, but must also keep up with those sandbaggers that somehow maintain their 20 handicaps and those scratch players that make fun of the easy course. So to even survive the ferocious battle of the links, the duffer must begin by paying close attention to the following rules of etiquette.

Slapping-the-mosquito
& other acceptable tactics

Loud burps or coughs during an opponent's backswing are just *too* obvious. Tapping a tee in irregular patterns or whispering to your partner are much more acceptable and skillful methods of throwing off an opponent's game. Of course, there is always the slapping-the-mosquito routine, but this must be reserved for extreme cases; for example, when you are one shot behind on the 18th during the club championship. Pretending to be partially deaf is another good tactic in distracting everyone's game. However, you had better not try this trick until you are over fifty.

Proper behavior
on the green

On the putting green the duffer can employ all sorts of neat tricks. Crossing fingers behind the back will hex most putts three feet and longer. Commenting on the speed of the green will also keep the opponent's ball from dropping into the hole. Remember, the duffer should only step on the line of the enemy's putt *after* the opponent has marked his ball; then the duffer will be less likely to attract attention when he accidently makes a spike mark on the path of the putting line.

Respecting your opponent
& helping him lose

Finally, the duffer must always be interested in his opponent's game, especially when it is plagued with mistakes. Commenting on bad shots in an understanding and sympathetic tone is a sure-fire method of keeping the opponent's game off and the duffer's on. Particularly good phrases to use are: "Gee, you didn't quite get all of that one, did you?" or "Too bad, just a little less slice and that would have been in-bounds," and "Boy, you sure had the line on that putt, but you know what they say . . . never up, never in."

Remember, the name of the game is *distraction* when it comes to duffer's etiquette and the fight to perpetuate his survival on the links.

DEFINITIONS

Duffer - any golfer with good intentions and mediocre results.

Mulligan - a duffer's best friend, not to be confused with a "gimmie" or the stew. The mulligan should be used whenever the duffer feels like using it.

Gimmie - any putt the duffer is sure he *cannot* make.

Sandbagger - a good golfer disguised as a duffer, or a dishonest duffer who only turns in his highest scores.

Duffers in Motion

Sand Trap - the duffer's play pen.

Divot - a secure resting place that a duffer provides for his opponent's ball.

Bunker - a famous TV hero.

Out-of-Bounds - a rude comment made by an opponent.

Waggle - the strange and mysterious movement the duffer makes with his club and body before hitting the ball. Some say the waggle originated as a ceremonious offering to the golf god; others speculate that it is a form of appeasement for missing church every Sunday.

Addressing the Ball - any time the duffer makes a poor shot, he will address the ball using all sorts of bad language.

Bad Lie - when a duffer says he has a 9 handicap, he is telling a bad lie.

In & Out - the fate of a duffer's good putt.

Yip - the fate of most of the duffer's putts.

The Waggle

Rub of the Green - a good excuse for hitting a bad shot. Also a phrase to use to describe an opponent's poor luck.

Fore - something to shout after the duffer is sure he has hit someone in his drive.

Teed off - the attitude of the golfer who has just been knocked unconscious by a duffer's drive.

Woods - clubs that the duffer cannot use and the place the duffer goes to look for his drives.

Handicap—the pride and peril of every duffer.

Triple Bogie—a score that's not too bad.

Double Bogie—a duffer's par.

Bogie —good score for the duffer.

Par—a duffer's dream.

Birdie—an impossible score for the duffer.

Eagle—an act of God.

Hole-in-One—are you kidding?

A Duffer's Biggest Handicap: Himself!

Windmill — the duffer's imitation of Dutch architecture.

Honor — something very difficult for the duffer to maintain during a round of golf.

Rules of Golf — items to be studied when the duffer is behind in a match.

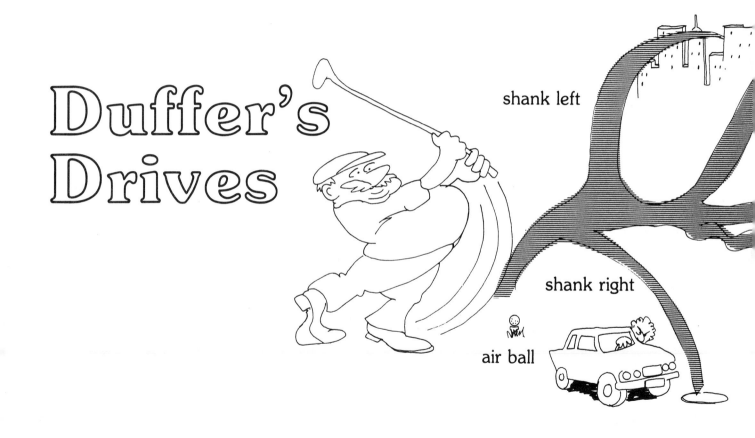

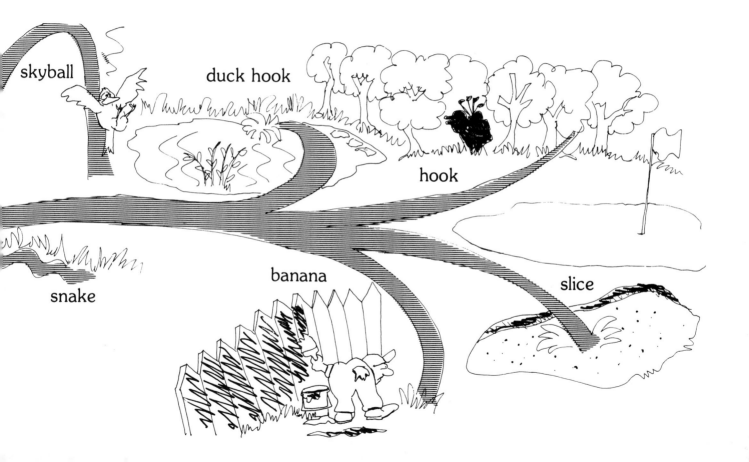

THE RULES

Rule 1 - The Game

(Viewed objectively, the game of golf is totally ridiculous, especially when the impartial observer follows the duffer in the height of battle on the links. After all who ever heard of grown men challenging one another to navigate a ball 1.68 inches in diameter and weighing 1.62 ounces, into a tiny hole 4.25 inches in diameter, sometimes 500 yards away, using equipment woefully inadequate for the chore? Therefore ...)

No duffer shall view the game of golf objectively.

Penalty for Breach of Rule: *Escort a carload of screaming Cub Scouts to a miniature golf course.*

Rule 2 — The Mulligan

(Every duffer should memorize this rule.) The mulligan, or "Now that's better" shot, shall be played whenever the dufter accidently hits a bad shot. The duffer and his partners know perfectly well that a dubbed shot is not planned and, in all fairness, should be played over.

Penalty for Breach of Rule: *Take a golf lesson.*

Rule 3 — The Gimmie

A gimmie shall be granted for any putt that a duffer can realistically make. In other words, a gimmie shall be granted for every putt under ten feet.

Penalty for Breach of Rule: *Spend one hour practicing putting.*

Rule 4 — Agreement to Waive Rules

The duffer may, without penalty, agree to waive any and all rules that would hinder the enjoyment of the game.

Penalty for Breach of Rule: *Ulcers.*

WEST DIVOT COURSE

HOLES	1	2	3	4	5	6	7	8	9	OUT
PAR	4	4	4	3	5	4	4	3	5	36
BLUE TEES	373	415	376	254	502	430	401	203	577	3531
WHITE TEES	300	400	300	200	400	330	300	100	450	2780
RED TEES	100	100	100	100	100	100	100	100	100	900
Joe Pro	4	4	4	3	5	4	4	3	5	36
Dan Duffer	6	6	8	4	7	7	6	5	5	54
Harry Hacker	7	8	8	5	7	6	8	7	8	63
Ned Novice	x	x	x	x	x	x	x	x	x	90

Rule 5—Counting Strokes

All strokes that the duffer can remember making during a round shall be recorded on the scorecard. Slips of memory are certainly understandable.

Penalty for Breach of Rule: *Serve a one-year term as chairman of the handicap committee.*

LOCAL RULES: Play fast. No lost balls. No. 5-out of bounds on Mrs. O'Leary's front porch. Replace sand blasted out of bunkers. Do not feed the alligators. Do not shoot the ducks. No beer consumption before the 15th hole. Thirty mph speed limit for golf carts. Skirts may not be worn in the club house after 10am.

Rule 6 — Ball Played as it Lies...in Unimprovable Situations.

The duffer shall play the ball as it lies. This is in order to avoid a penalty stroke. (Duffers shall view this as one of the cardinal rules of the game.)

Penalty for Breach of Rule: *Spend one morning retrieving balls on the driving range.*

Rule 7 — Discontinuance of Play

The duffer shall never, never cease a round of golf, under *any* circumstances.

Penalty for Breach of Rule: *Spend three weekends at home mowing the lawn and emptying the garbage.*

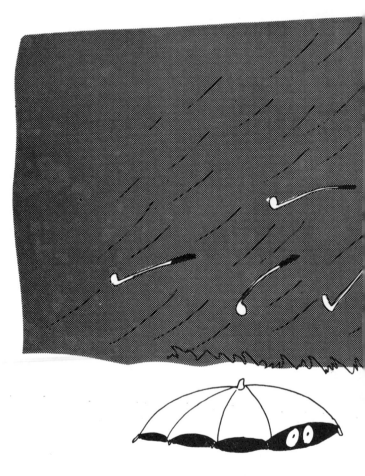

Rule 8 — Obstructions

The duffer shall be prepared to move any and all obstructions that unjustly impair his stance, swing or line of vision.

Penalty for Breach of Rule: *Serve one weekend on the grounds crew.*

Rule 9—Preferred Lies

The duffer shall make preferred lies only when they advance his chances of winning the match.

Penalty for Breach of Rule: *Play against the Chairman of the Rules Committee.*

Rule 10 — Relief from Casual Water

A duffer may take relief from casual water by proceeding:

a) *Through the green* to the nearest point from where his ball lies to a secluded spot not more than halfway to the next tee.

b) *In a hazard* a duffer shall take relief from casual water only after having sunk waist-deep in the hazard.

Penalty for Breach of Rule: *Play golf with the whole family for three weekends.*

Rule 11-Winter Rules

Winter rules shall be in effect at all times, especially during the summer.

Penalty for Breach of Rule: *Give opponent a seven stroke advantage.*

Rule 12 — Ground Under Repair

A duffer shall deem as ground under repair any surface that his ball lies in that would make for an unusually difficult shot.

Penalty for Breach of Rule: *Join the Optimist's Club.*

Rule 13—Superstitions Allowed
There shall be no Rule 13. It would be unlucky.

Penalty for Breach of Rule: *Loss of good-luck ball marker for one round.*

Rule 14—Delay of Play

A duffer upon losing a hole may pause before resuming play to:

    a) utter profanities at the top of his lungs
    b) send his caddie to the pro shop for new balls
    c) pour another martini from the thermos on his golf cart
    d) wrap his putter around the nearest tree.

Penalty for Breach of Rule: *Swim with frogs in the nearest lily pond.*

Rule 15—Lost Ball

A duffer shall never lose a golf ball. A substitute ball rolling accidently out of the hand and into the rough will be allowed.

Penalty for Breach of Rule: *Resume playing with a marshmallow.*

Rule 16—Disputes, Decisions and Doubts

If there be any disputes, difficult decisions, or doubts that arise during play, a foursome shall shout loudly, call names, swear, and pout.

Penalty for Breach of Rules: *Join a new golf club.*

50

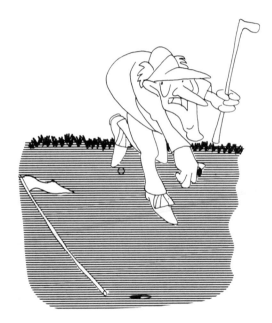

Rule 17—Marking the Ball on the Putting Green

A ball shall be marked on the surface using the following procedure: Place the marker three inches in front of *the ball*, remove the ball, and replace the ball three inches in front of *the marker*.

Penalty for Breach of Rule: *Take three strokes to putt out.*

Rule 18—Hazards

When in a sand trap or other similar hazard, the duffer shall consider his ball to be in a footprint. He is then entitled to smooth out the "footprint" and place the ball so that it can be putted and not blasted out of the hazard.

Penalty for Breach of Rule: *Keep sand in shoes for rest of the round.*

Rule 19 — Out-of-Bounds

The duffer shall feign color blindness when hitting a ball out-of-bounds. A white out-of-bounds marker shall only be recognized when an opponent's ball is out-of-bounds.

Penalty for Breach of Rule: *Have eyes checked.*

Rule 20 — Ball Unfit for Play

The ball may be deemed unfit for play whenever it is lost, hit into a water hazard, or is dubbed. The duffer shall replace the unfit ball with one that is bright, shiny, new and luckier.

Penalty for Breach of Rule: *Take your ball to the health spa.*

58

Rule 21 — Searching for a Lost Ball

Search for a lost ball may last no longer than 10 seconds (in the case of a duffer looking for his opponent's ball) or 10 minutes (in the case of a duffer trying to find his own ball). This rule shall be strictly enforced by the foursome who are waiting on the preceding tee.

Penalty for Breach of Rule: *Concussion from a ball hit by impatient duffer on the preceding tee.*

Rule 22—Attitude towards Joggers on Golf Course

All duffers, upon spotting a jogger on the course, shall make every attempt to discourage the jogger from ever darkening the links with his sweaty presence again.

Penalty for Breach of Rule: *Jog one mile around the golf course.*

Rule 23—Identifying the Ball

A duffer must make absolutely certain he identifies his ball, especially when it lies in the rough. If, when replacing the ball in its original position, it happens to roll into the fairway, so much the better.

Penalty for Breach of Rule: *Play the next round with a florescent orange golf ball.*

Rule 24 — Appropriate Language during Play

Every attempt should be made to spare opponents and partners the indignity of abusive language. The duffer should only swear in muffled tones similar to: "Muh-Fuh-Sun-Beach."

Penalty for Breach of Rule: *Play one round with your mother-in-law.*

Rule 25 — Throwing Golf Clubs

The duffer should only throw his golf clubs when he feels he can throw them farther than he has hit the ball. In such a case he should play his next shot from the position of the farthest club.

Penalty for Breach of Rule: *Hit next shot with the golf bag.*

Rule 26—Interference from an Outside Agency

If a ball comes to rest on a moving outside agency, the duffer shall follow in hot pursuit. Exception: when the ball comes to rest on a bee hive, in the mouth of a mad dog, or on the back of an alligator.

Penalty for Breach of Rule: *One week in traction.*

Rule 27 — Being Hit (or Nearly Hit) by Ball

In the event that a duffer is accidently hit by another duffer's ball, he shall be entitled to:

    a) throw the ball into the nearest water hazard

    b) put the ball into his bag and walk off with it

    c) replace ball with an ostrich egg

Penalty for Breach of Rule: *Apologize to the duffer whose ball hit you.*

68

Rule 28—Practicing

The duffer shall never, never, never practice his game.

Penalty for Breach of Rule: *Assume a 7 handicap for life and never win a match again.*

Rule 29 — Making a Hole-in-One

Upon making a hole-in-one, the duffer shall be required to buy drinks for everyone in the clubhouse.

Penalty for Breach of Rule: *Be thrown into the nearest water hazard.*

Rule 30—Advice and Reminiscing
The duffer shall never give advice or recount golf stories to others in his foursome unless asked to do so.

Penalty for Breach of Rule: *Play four Sundays as a singleton, you simpleton.*

Rule 31—Maximum of Fourteen balls

The duffer shall use no more than 14 balls during a round of golf except in the following cases:

>   a) playing a course with more than three water holes
>   b) when his caddy is a used ball salesman
>   c) when playing with his spouse (in which case he will be allowed one ball per hole, providing that both parties are consenting and there is no appreciable delay of play).

Penalty for Breach of Rule: *Use one ball for the rest of the round.*

Rule 32—Bird Feather Rule

If a bird in flight is hit by the duffer's ball, the duffer shall be entitled to play his shot again. However, the duffer must produce evidence in the form of a bird's feather and will hold it up calling, "Bird Feather Rule!"

Exception: a ball shall be played where it lies after coming in contact with an American bald eagle or other endangered species.

Penalty for Breach of Rule: *Hit the next shot with a bird feather.*

Rule 33—On the Putting Green

As putting is a particularly nerve-wracking and embarrassing part of the game, the duffer may use any and all devices to insure successful results.

Penalty for Breach of Rule: *Hit the next five putts blindfolded.*

Rule 34—Striking at the Ball

The ball shall be struck at fairly with the clubhead except when putting within 24 inches of the hole. In this case the duffer may push the ball directly into the hole.

Penalty for Breach of Rule: *Hit next putt with a baseball bat.*

Appendix I — Proper Dress on the Golf Course

A well dressed duffer is a sight to behold. "Gaudy" is the key word when it comes to picking a wardrobe. The purpose of golf dress, besides covering up the atrophied muscles of an almost "well-tuned" athlete, is to distract one's opponent. A shocking purple shirt can subtly irritate the eyes of a more conservative duffer. Wildly checkered pants will, if positioned correctly, confuse any opponent trying to line up a shot. Of course, two-or three-toned golf shoes, pink golf glove and striped socks will do wonders to improve the duffers chances of winning.

Classic Dress — Of course, if the duffer wishes to dress more conservatively, he may assume the attire of the Classic Duffer. It should be noted, too, that any duffer over the age of ninety is *required* to wear the Classic Duffer's garb. A thinly striped shirt with knitted tie and a V-necked sweater form the basic attire for this experienced duffer. More importantly, the Classic Duffer should not forget a good pair of knickers and sporty knee socks, argyle of course. The two-toned golf shoes are also a must, as well as the large driving cap. In this classic habiliment the duffer will be mistaken for a retired professional and intimidate any gullible opponent.

Dress for Foul Weather—Same as dress for normal occasions except with the addition of light blue rain gear and a multi-colored umbrella. Optional accessories include an inflatable rubber raft, a portable lighting rod, and snow tires for the golf cart.

Dress for Hot Weather — Same as normal dress but with shorts, madras if possible, and argyle knee socks.

Dress for Cold Weather — Same as normal dress except with the addition of a chartreuse V-necked sweater with insignia, a yellow wind breaker, thermal underwear, special golf gloves, ear muffs, and the special orange-colored golf ball for playing in snow.

Appendix II—Handicaps

The duffer has nothing more important than his handicap. When asked the question, "What are you?" the duffer should not reply "Presbyterian," "Jew," or "Catholic," but rather "22," "16," or "30." Although not necessarily proud of his handicap, a duffer must, nevertheless, cherish it. A well-kept handicap can mean untold rewards at the end of a lucky round or even a mediocre one. Inconsistency is the guideline for the duffer who wants to keep his modestly high handicap. The duffer must not become too greedy with a handicap that allows continual winning. No, that would only lead to his demise and eventual delegation to the ranks of the "good golfer."

Appendix III — Policy on Gambling

Betting is one of the primary thrills of golfing. There is no excitement to match investing money on something so unpredictable. Duffers especially like gambling because everyone can win... anyone can get lucky. The fact that skill has so little to do with the outcome of a golf bet is why, it is believed, so many duffers are willing to play any and all bets. It is recommended, therefore, that the duffer bet as much and as often as his bankroll will allow.

The duffer should bet on the outcome of the total match, and on the outcome of each hole. A bet on the number of putts is also appropriate, as well as the number of fairways reached safely or otherwise. Of course, there are "greenies" on the par threes if the duffer thinks he can actually reach the green, and longest drive competitions for the muscle duffers.

If the duffer should become bored with these means of losing his money, he may bet on totally unrelated things, such as the number of beers he can consume during an 18-hole match. Or, if it is a particularly slow day on the links, an on-the-tee craps game should be arranged.

Appendix IV — Sizing Up the Opponent

A duffer will meet all sorts of opponents on the course. He must be able to recognize each type so he may plan the appropriate strategy for winning. The following will describe various types of golfers and suggest methods of out-witting them in the battle of the links.

The Hacker — not to be confused with the duffer, the hacker is easily identified by his cut-off shorts, white socks, dirty white tee shirt, six-pack of beer, and fifty-year old clubs. It will not be difficult to beat the hacker because he does not play enough to have a handicap and is, therefore, more optimistic about his skill than he should be. The only strategy in playing the hacker is to bet as much money as possible and wait for the 18th hole to collect the bet.

The Novice — is also easily identified. He will be wearing brand new golf shoes that squeak and are so stiff that he will bob up and down when he walks. The novice will be young and inexperienced and should not be taken advantage of unless he begins to brag about his low scores. If this happens, the duffer should proceed as if playing the hacker.

The Scratch Player — is recognized by his simply colored outfit and, most importantly, by the extreme look of confidence on his face. He will be telling stories about the time he scored a 70 at St. Andrews and will be ignoring everyone but other scratch golfers. The strategy to beating this egomaniac is to use the handicap to its fullest. The fact is that the scratch player never gets a handicap, so rub in the fact that he has to play three of four under par to win. This technique will win the duffer a handsome bet and keep the scratch player from visiting the course again.

The Chairman of the Rules Committee — the duffer will recognize this golfer by his perfect behavior, pristine clothes, and complete lack of personality. The duffer must be in top form to beat this opponent, being particularly careful when following the Official Duffer's Rules as they might occasionally conflict with those the chairman follows. The duffer must be especially careful to play his shot when the Chairman is not looking. In his zealous attempt to keep track of the duffer's score, the Chairman will forget his own game and probably fall to pieces after the first nine. So the duffer should place a large bet on the second nine.

The Aggressive Player — is identified by the look of stress and deep thought that is ever-present in his face. The duffer must be careful not to arouse the aggressive golfer as it will probably mean a trip to the hospital. The strategy in playing this type of golfer is to hit the ball as far away from his ball as possible. Let him defeat himself and watch out for flying golf clubs. It is advisable not to bet anything when playing this golfer; but if he insists, bet as little as possible, and of course, never, ever try to collect any winnings.

The Gambler— is recognized by his cowboy-boot golf shoes, his ten gallon golf cap and his Rolls Royce golf cart. The duffer must be especially careful when taking on the gambler in head-to-head competiton. If possible, bet one hole at a time. This way the duffer will be able to determine what kind of golfer this character really is, behind all the paraphernalia.

The Professional — the duffer will probably never see the professional anywhere near the course, but the pro is easily recognized if the duffer happens to see him. The pro will be dressed casually but tastefully and will be playing a totally different type of golf. The duffer should never make a wager with a professional! The pro will always win. It is better to engage in pleasant conversation and comment on how good he was in the last televised tournament.

The Long Hitter — is usually at least six feet tall. As he warms up notice he will swing the club hard and extremely fast. He will be dressed in clothes that are a tad too small for him because he is still growing. The long hitter can be beaten by simply saying, on the first tee and after he has hit a 300 yard drive, "Gee, you're not quite hitting them as far today." That will throw off his whole game and the duffer will be sure to collect a nice sum at the end of the day.

Sizing Up The Caddie

Perhaps one of the more important skills the duffer should develop is the ability to size up the caddie when approaching the first tee. How the duffer can use his caddie will often determine how well the duffer will play. There are three basic types of caddies and the following descriptions will help the duffer size up the caddie when playing a round.

The Eager Beaver—this caddie is easily recognized by the fact that the duffer will not be able to see this caddie because he is shorter than the golf bag. Often he will be carrying two bags, in which case all that will ever will be seen will be two bags moving mysteriosly down the fairway. The eager beaver is best used by the duffer as a bag holder. The duffer should carry most of the clubs himself. This way, play will not be slowed down and the little fellow will not have his feelings hurt.

The Ancient Mariner — this caddie has been around for a long time. The duffer will recognize him by the long white hair and the tatoos on each arm. The Ancient Mariner will come in handy when the duffer is trying to choose the right club on a difficult hole. However, the duffer should listen for coughs and wheezes as approaching the tee — a warning to get out the ear plugs. This trait is the only draw back of the ancient mariner.

The Pro's Son — this caddie is clean shaven (if he has any beard at all), blond, athletic, and confident looking. If lucky enough to get the pro's son as a caddie, the duffer should be sure to send Arnie Jr. ahead to look for balls that go into the woods. Don't let him become bored or he will make fun of the duffer's game . . . this caddie usually has about an 8 handicap.

Appendix VI—Taking a Lesson

In general, the duffer should avoid taking lessons. However, if the urge strikes — beware. The idea of a lesson is to learn by accident rather than on purpose. Everyone knows that a golf lesson can ruin a duffer's game (not that there is much to ruin). The phrase "analysis leads to paralysis" is one that is especially apt for duffer golf. Therefore, when taking a lesson, the duffer should do exactly what the pro tells him to do and then try to forget everything as soon as the lesson is over. Keeping notes and trying to be a good pupil will only get the duffer into trouble. Remember, once a duffer, always a duffer.